Enchanted Flowers

A coloring book with floral designs

Queenie Wong

ISBN-13: 978-1535076630
ISBN-10: 1535076631
First published in United States in 2016
Illustrations by Queenie Wong
Wonger0050@yahoo.com.hk

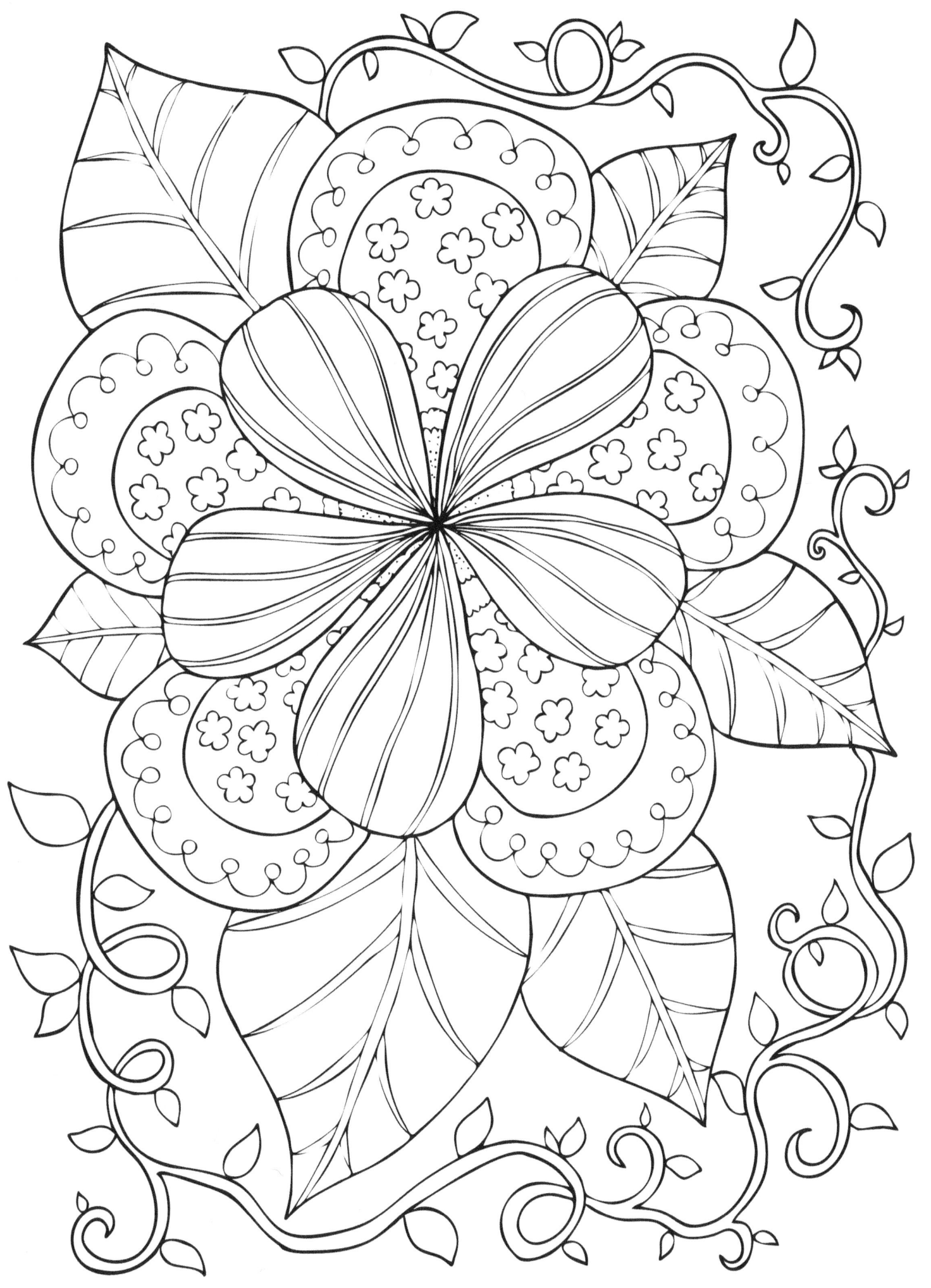

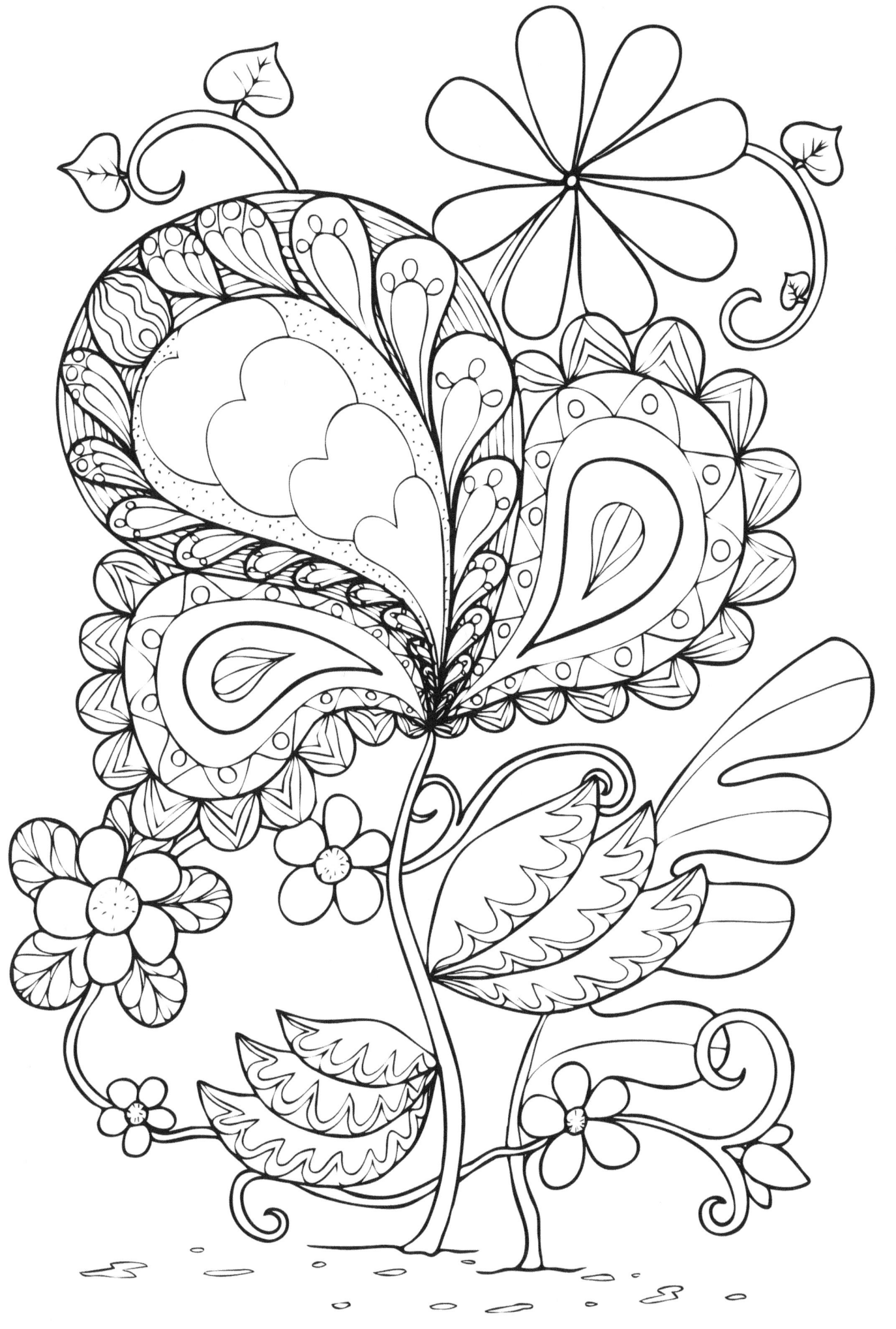

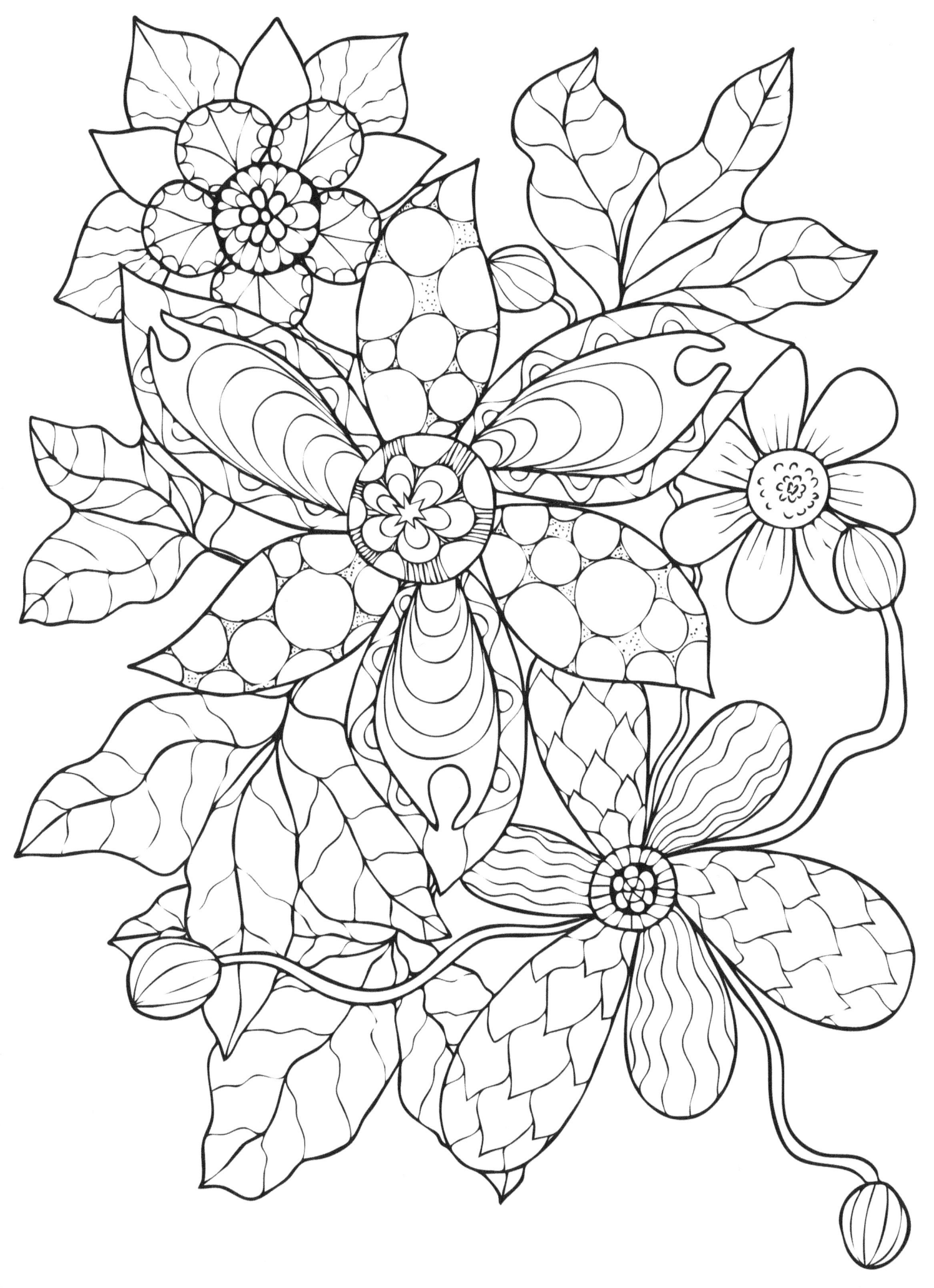

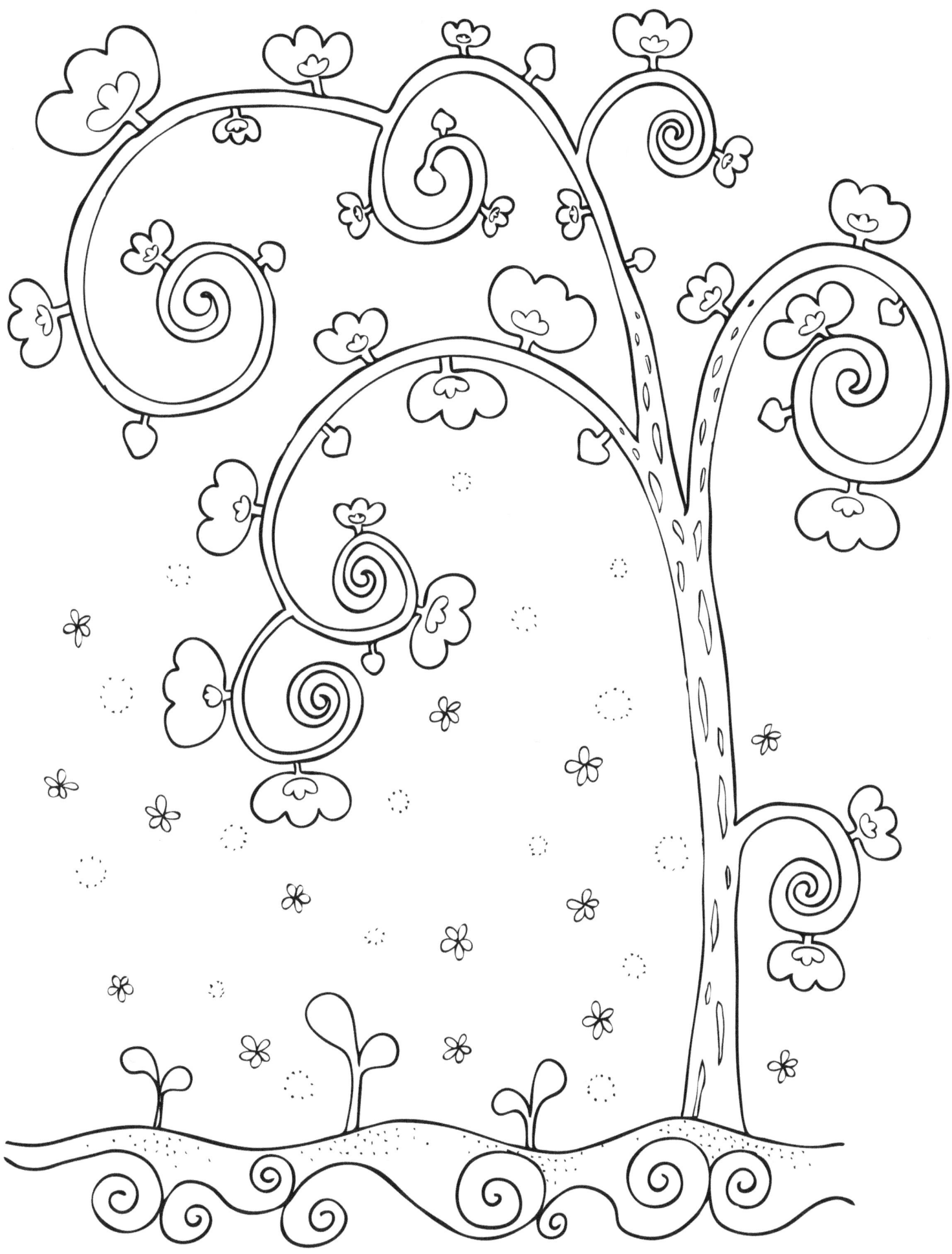

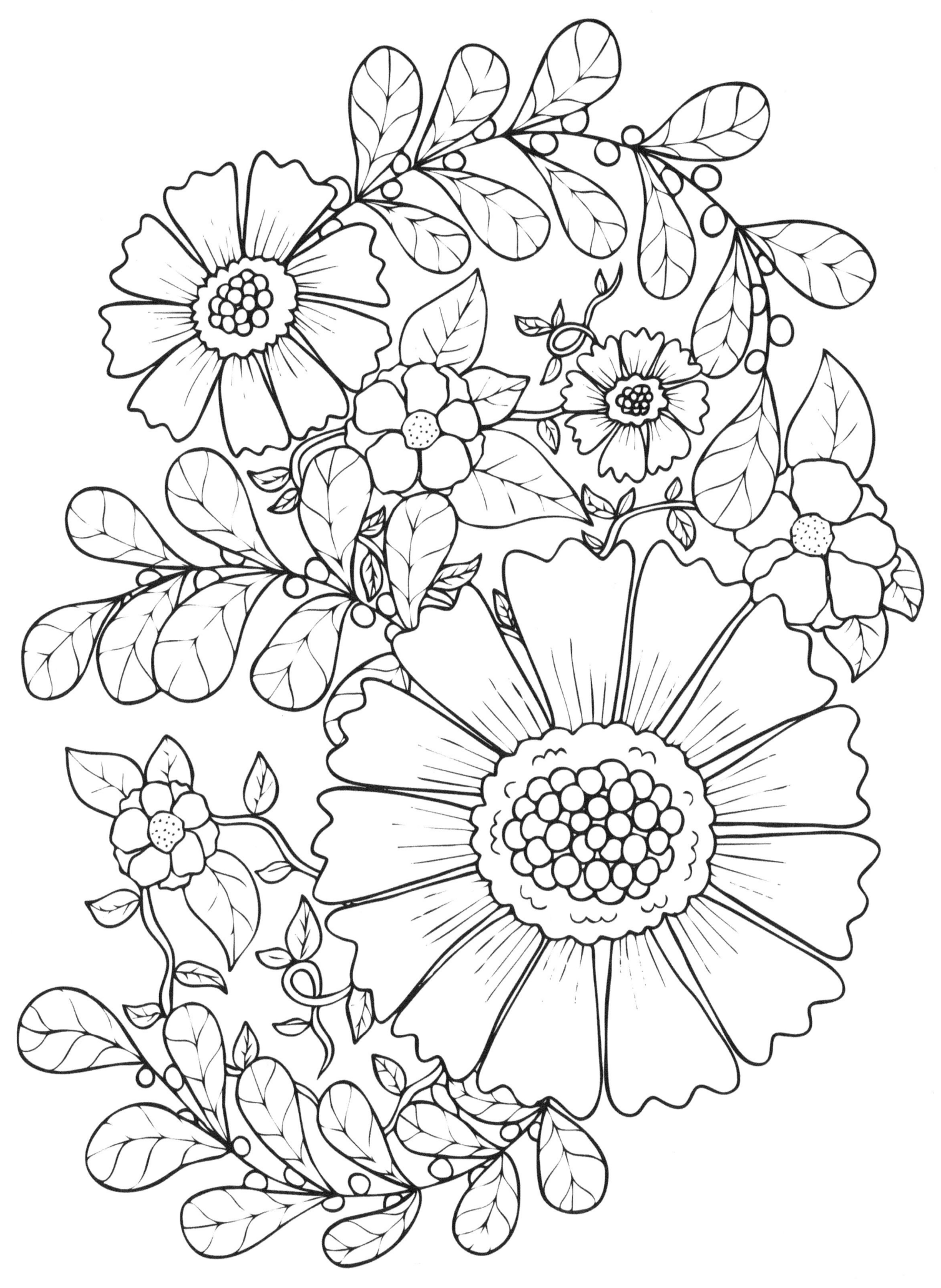

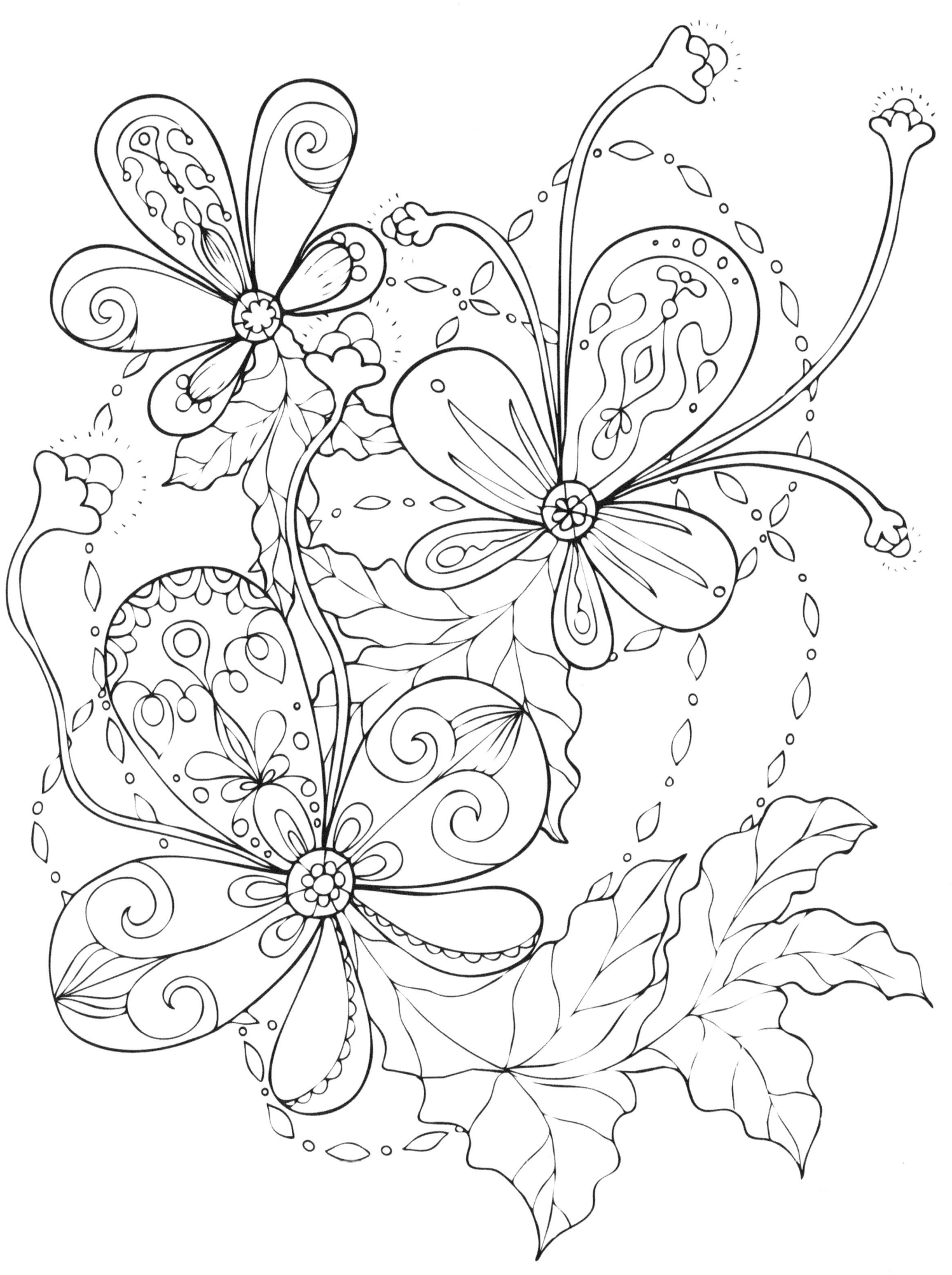

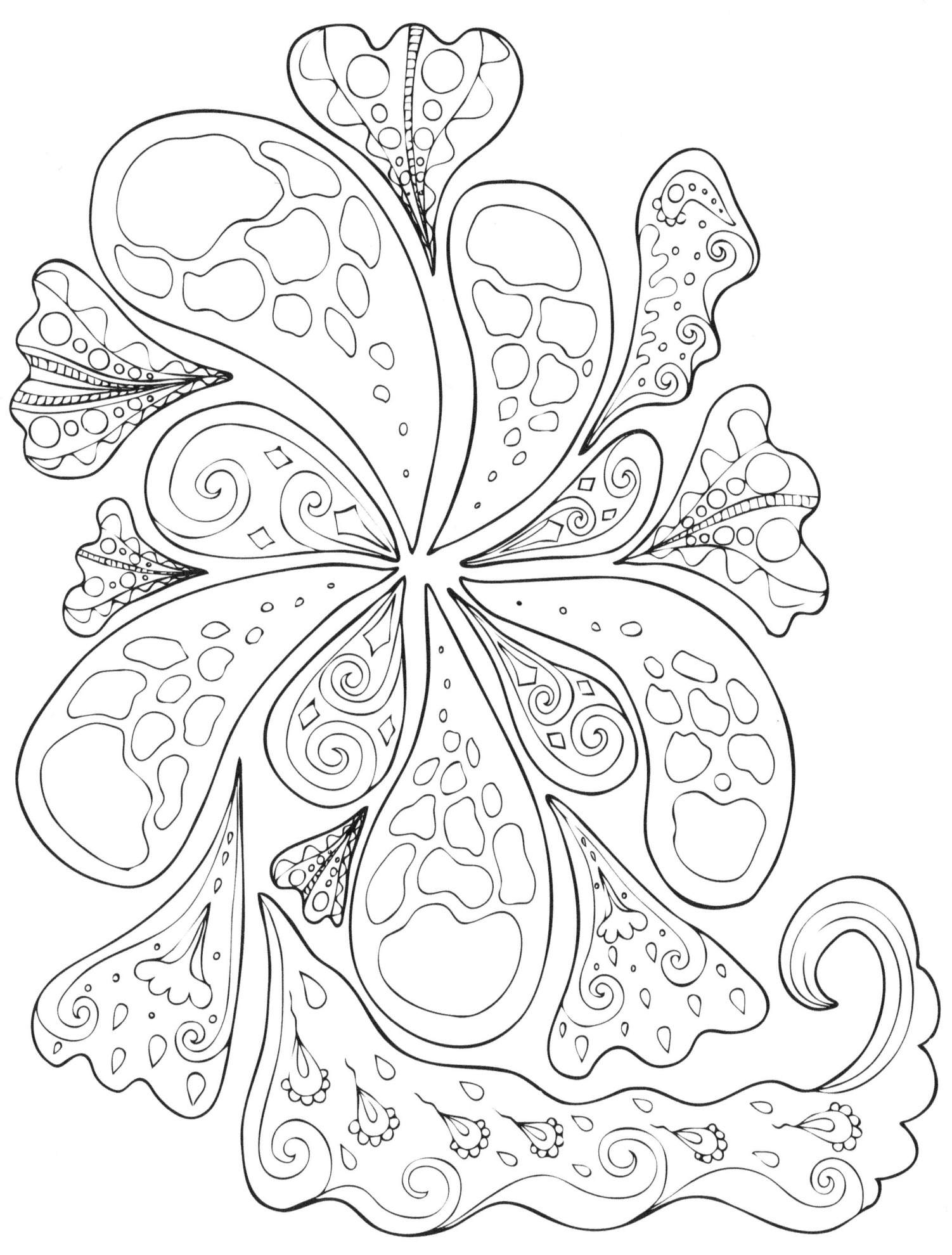

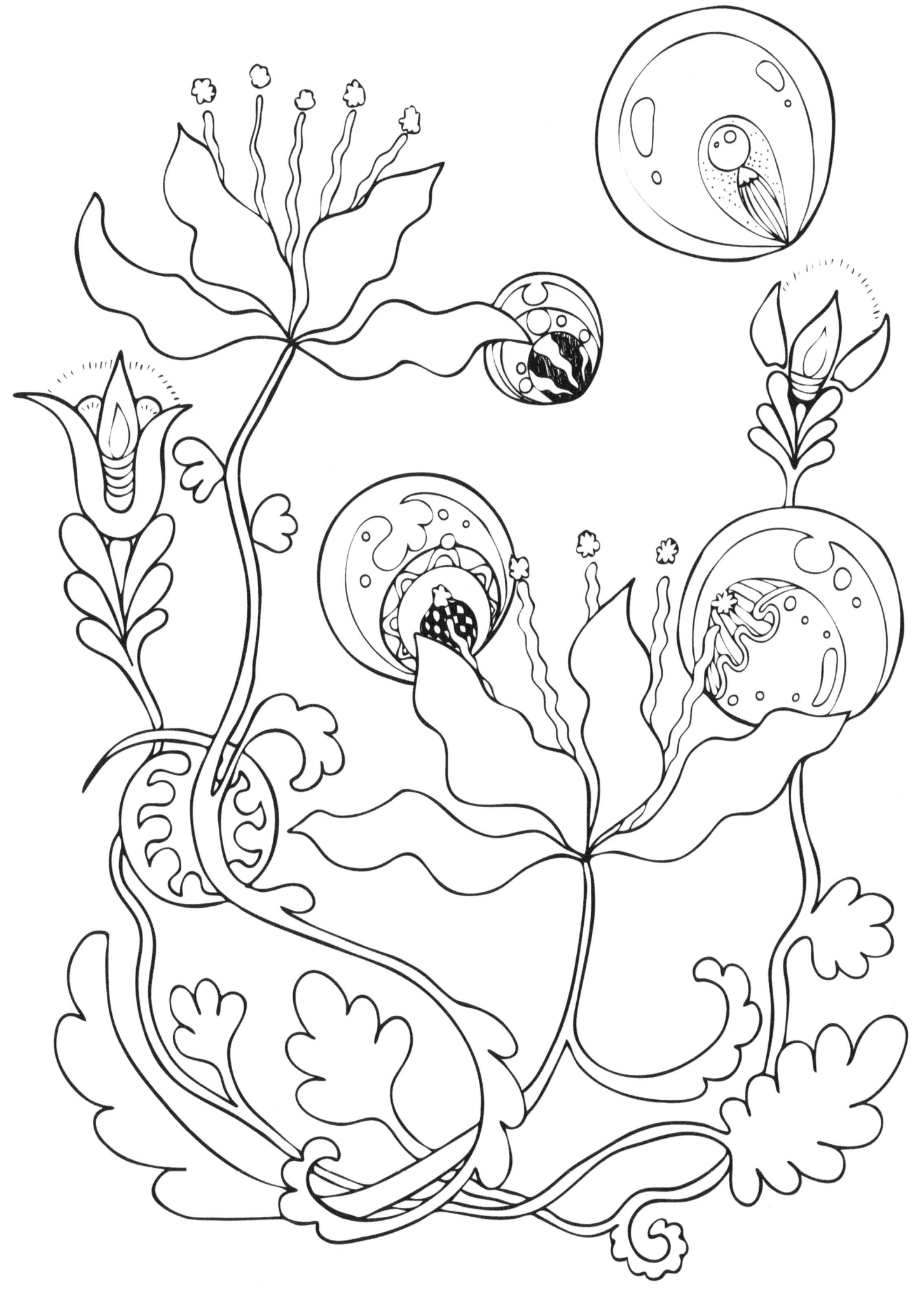

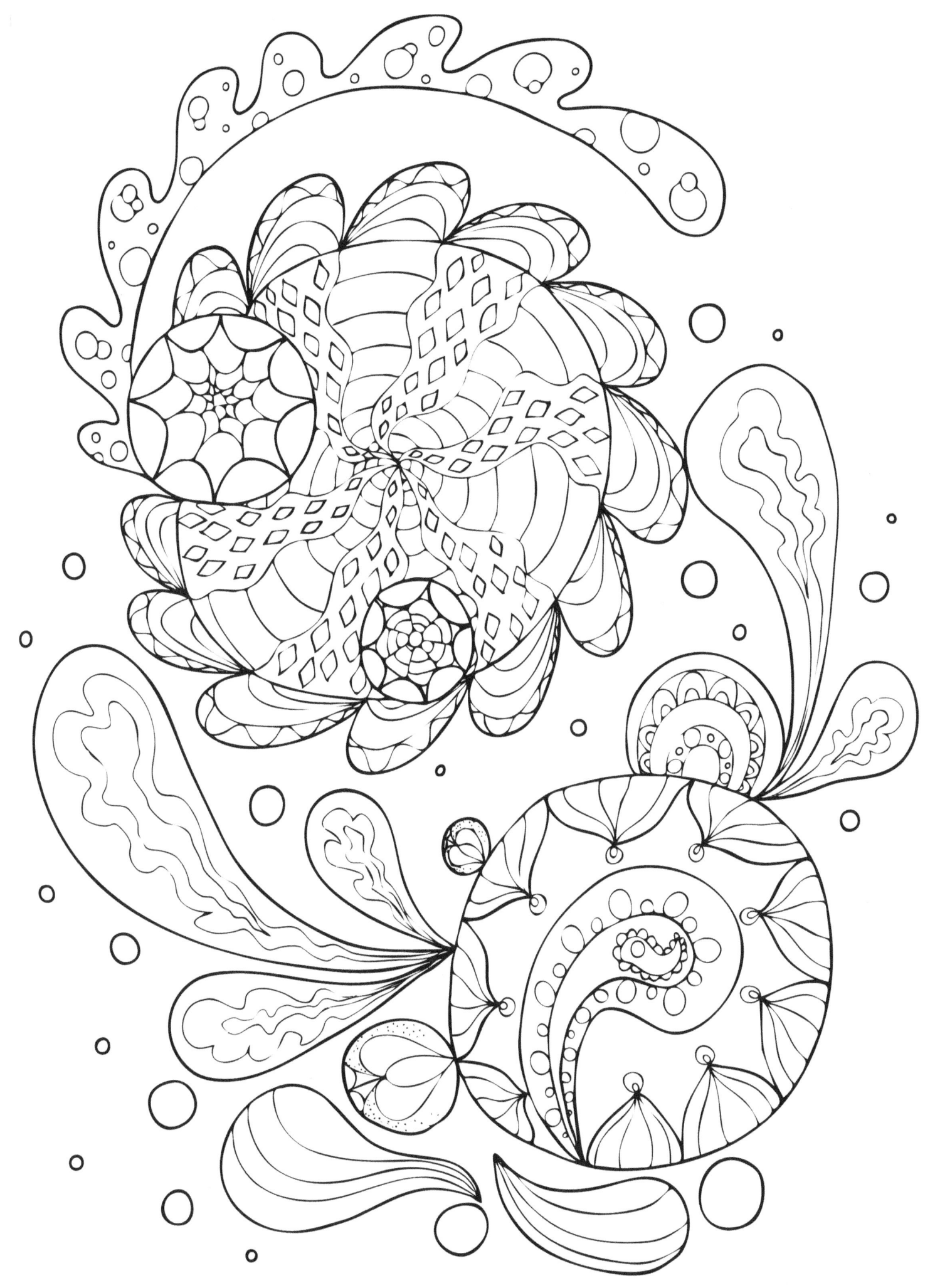

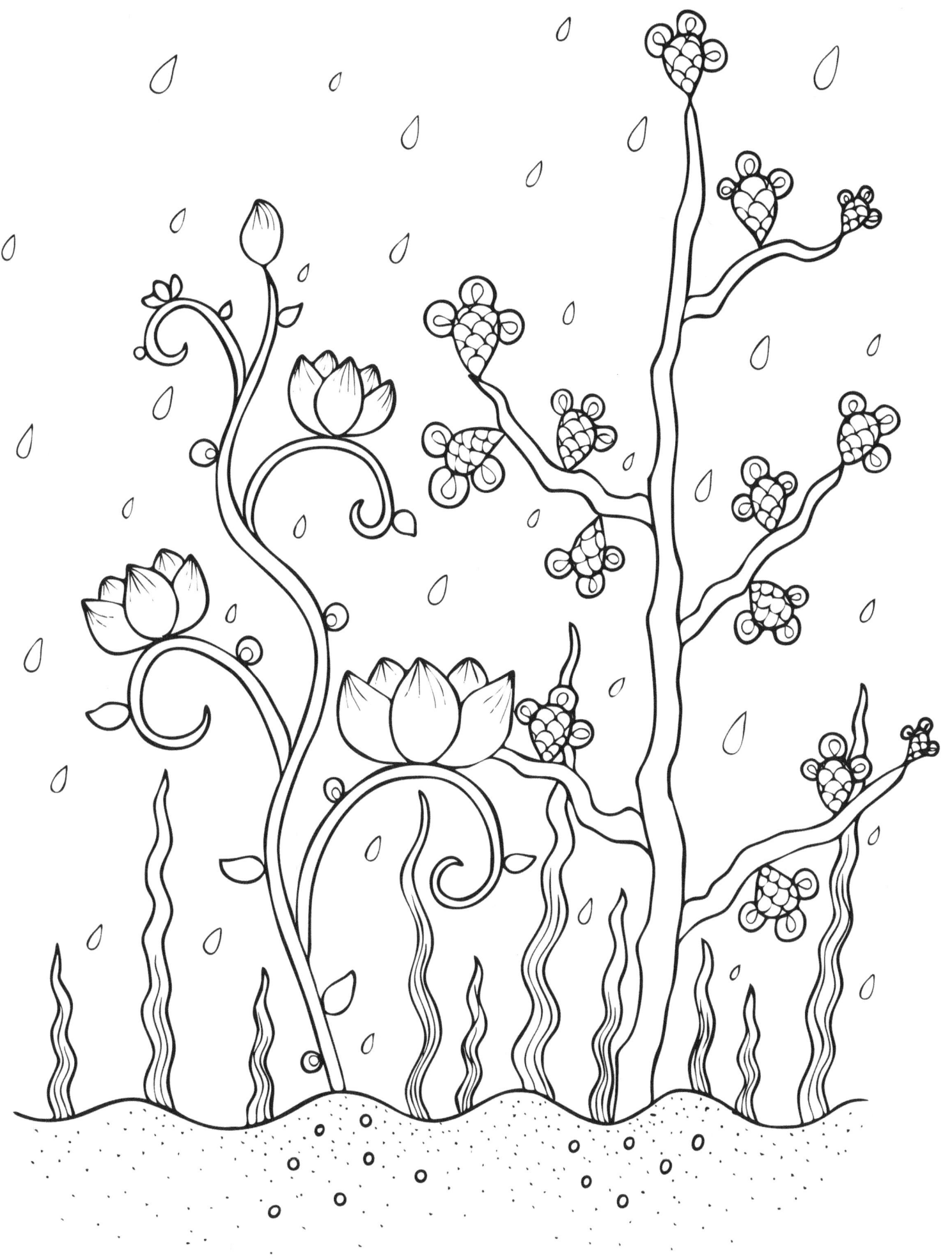

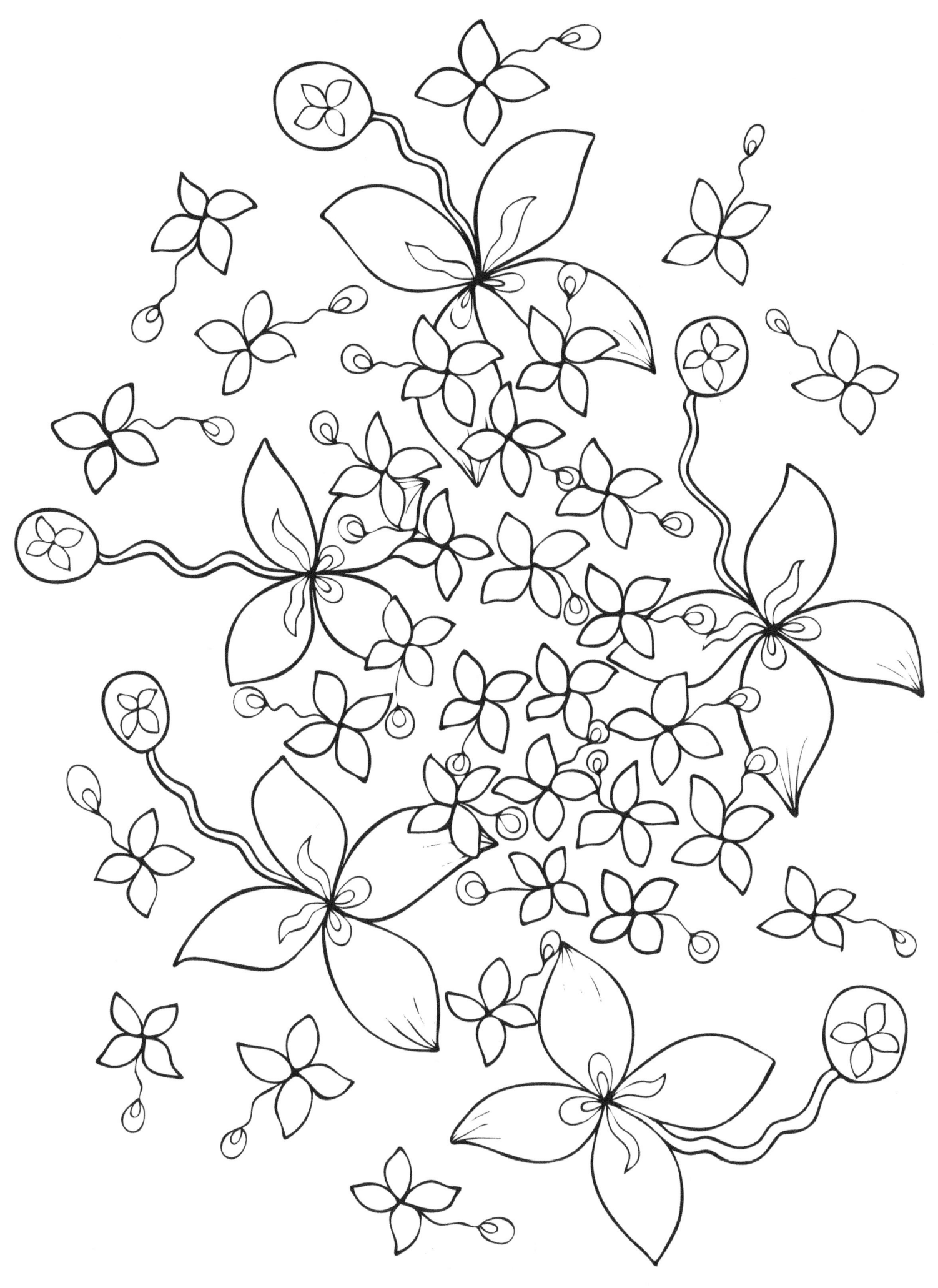

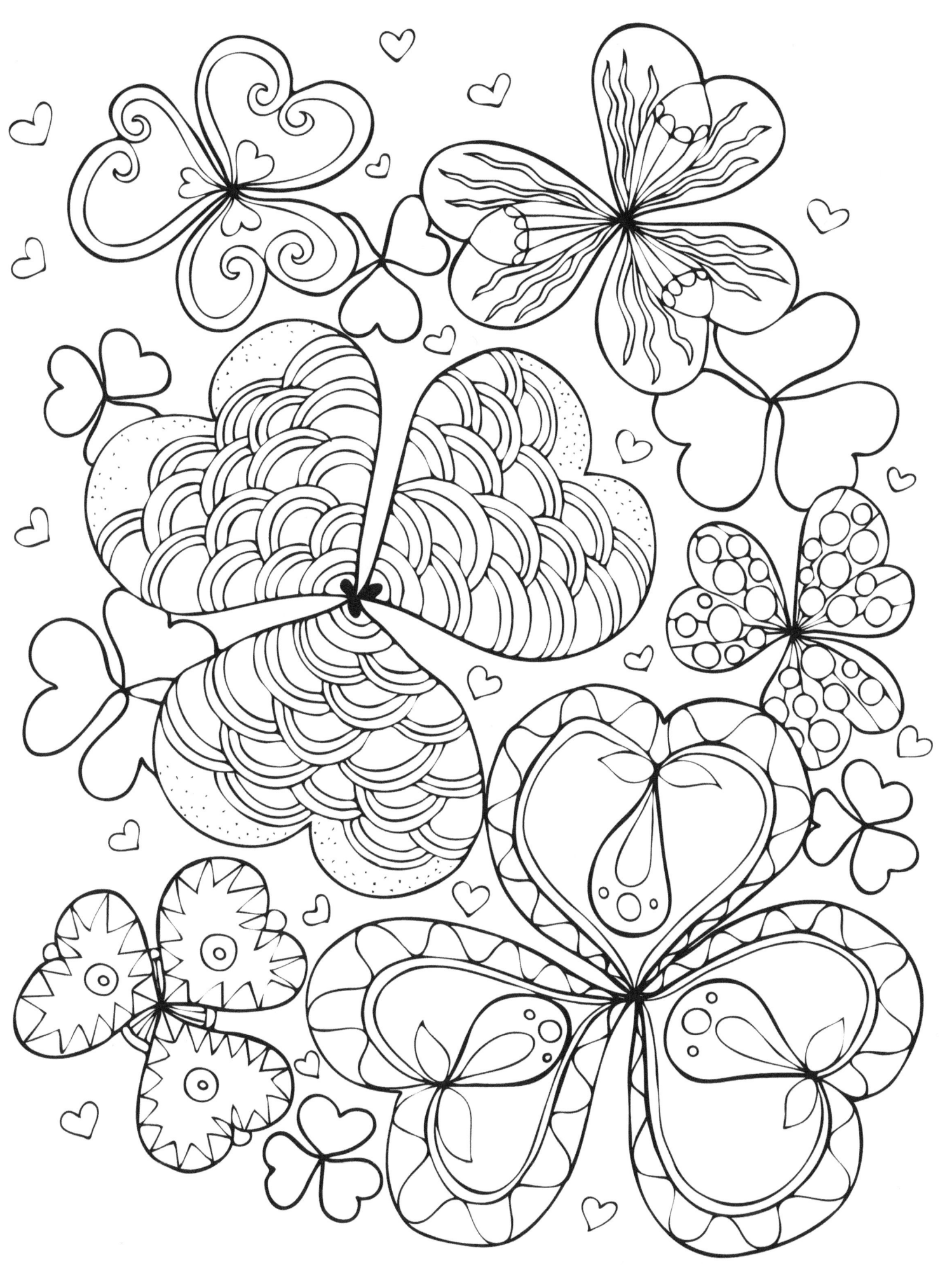

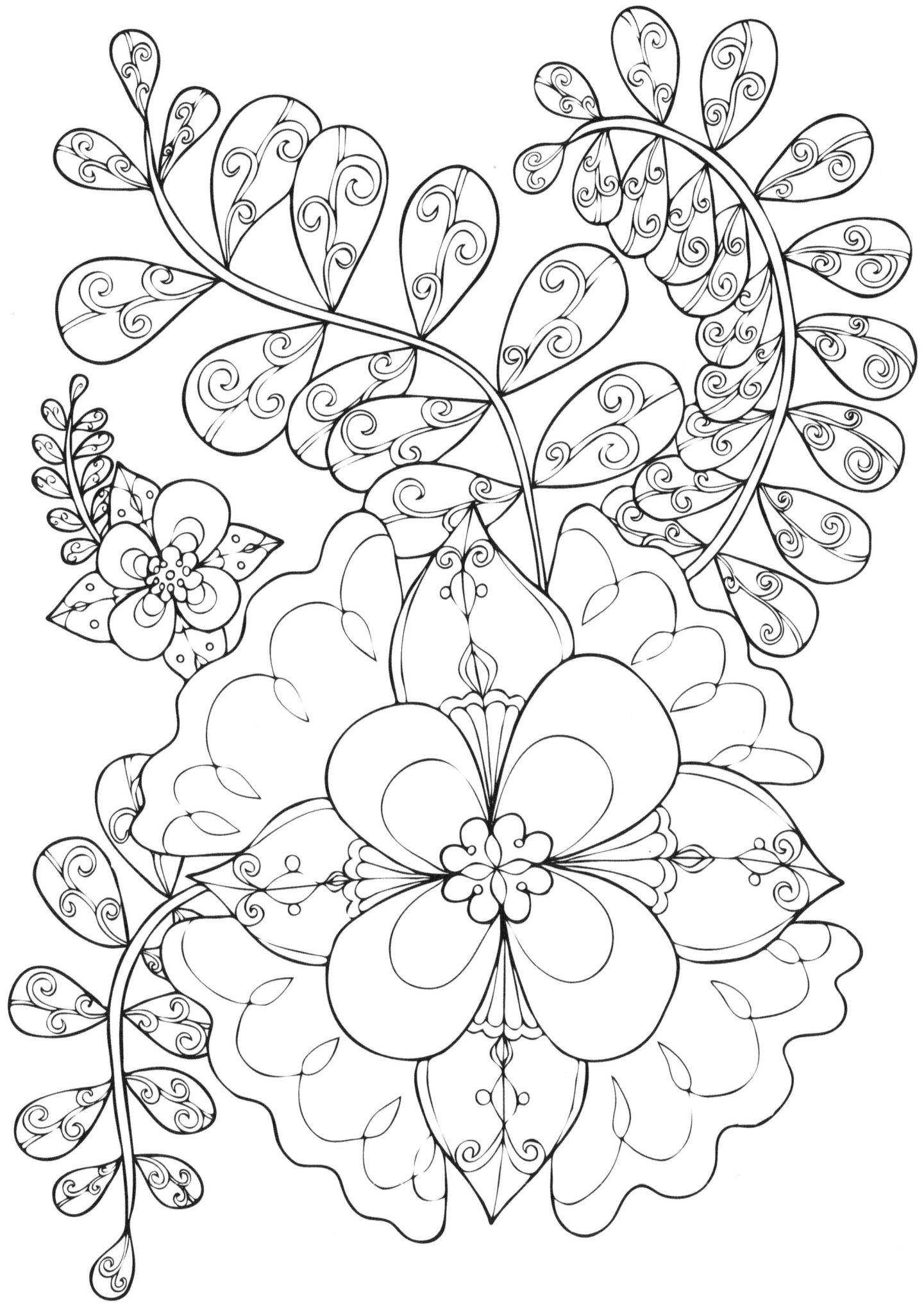

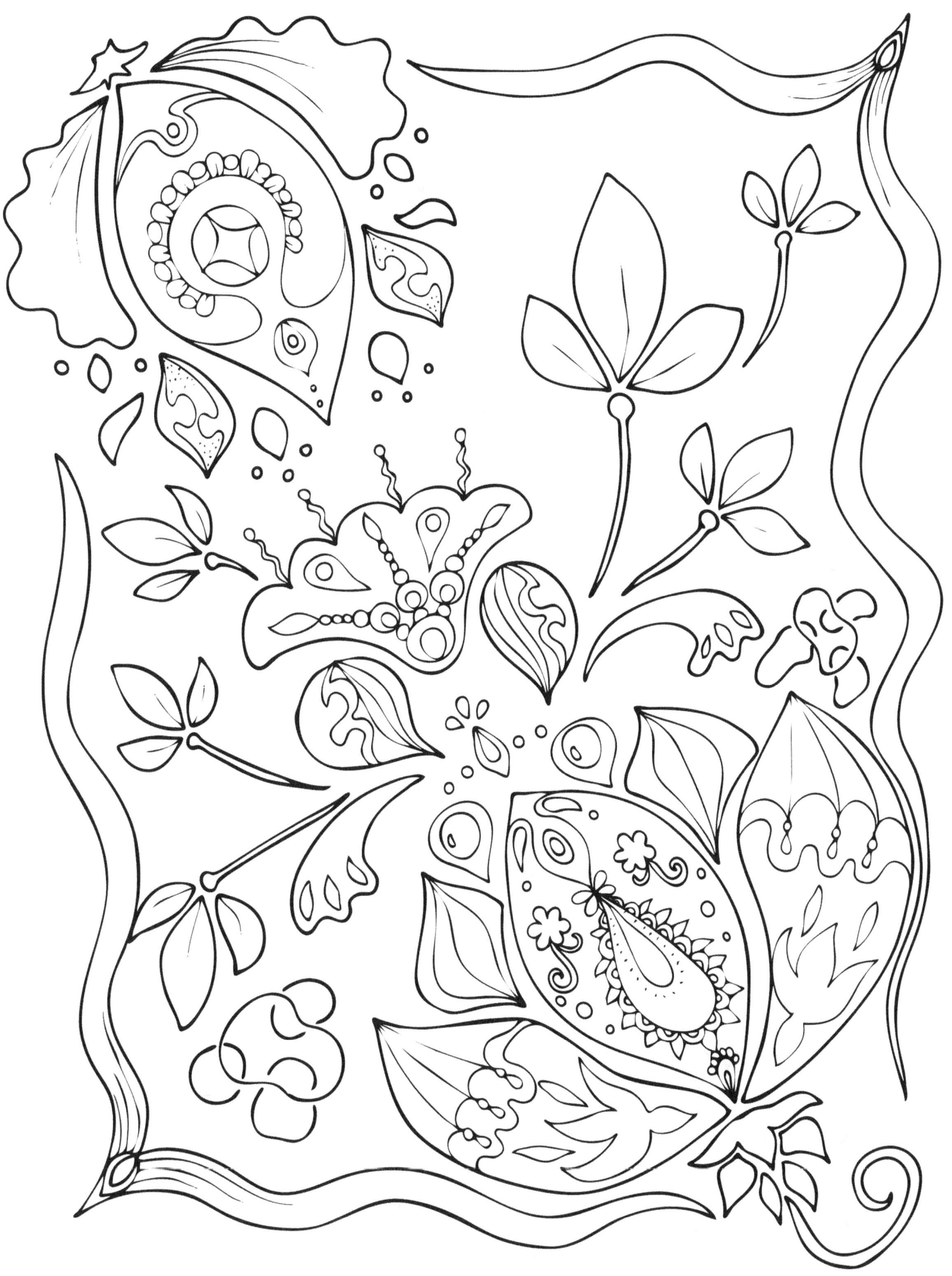

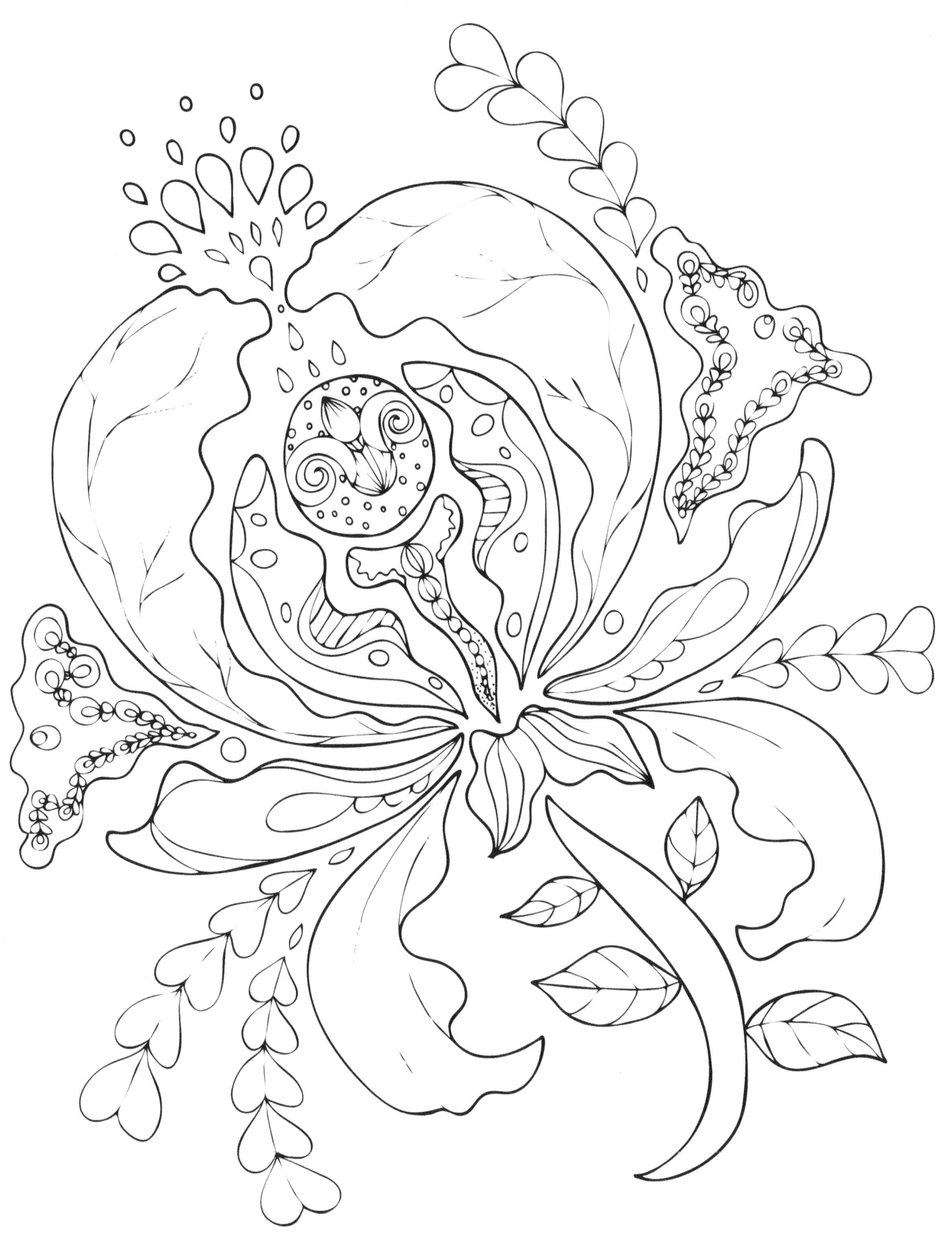

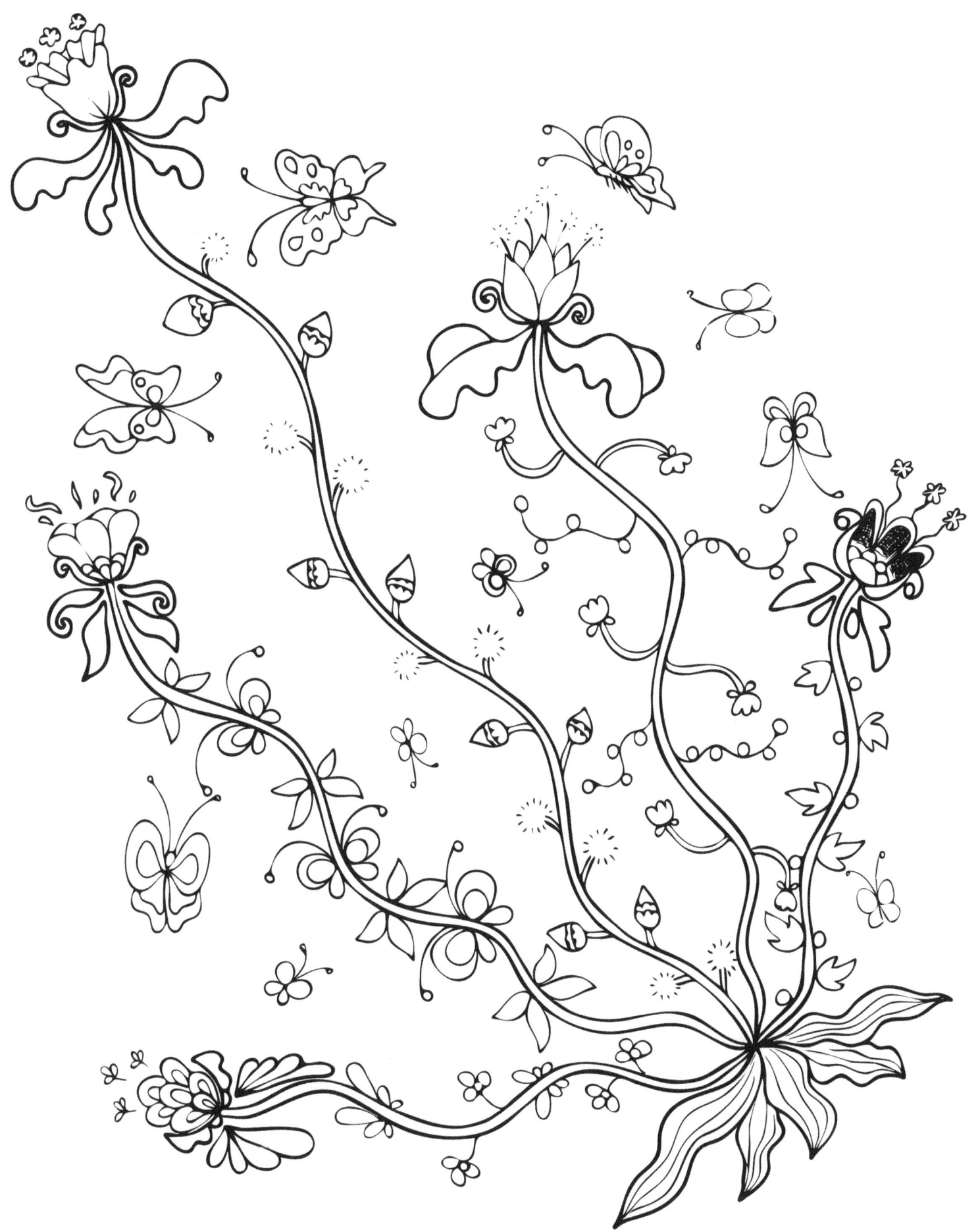

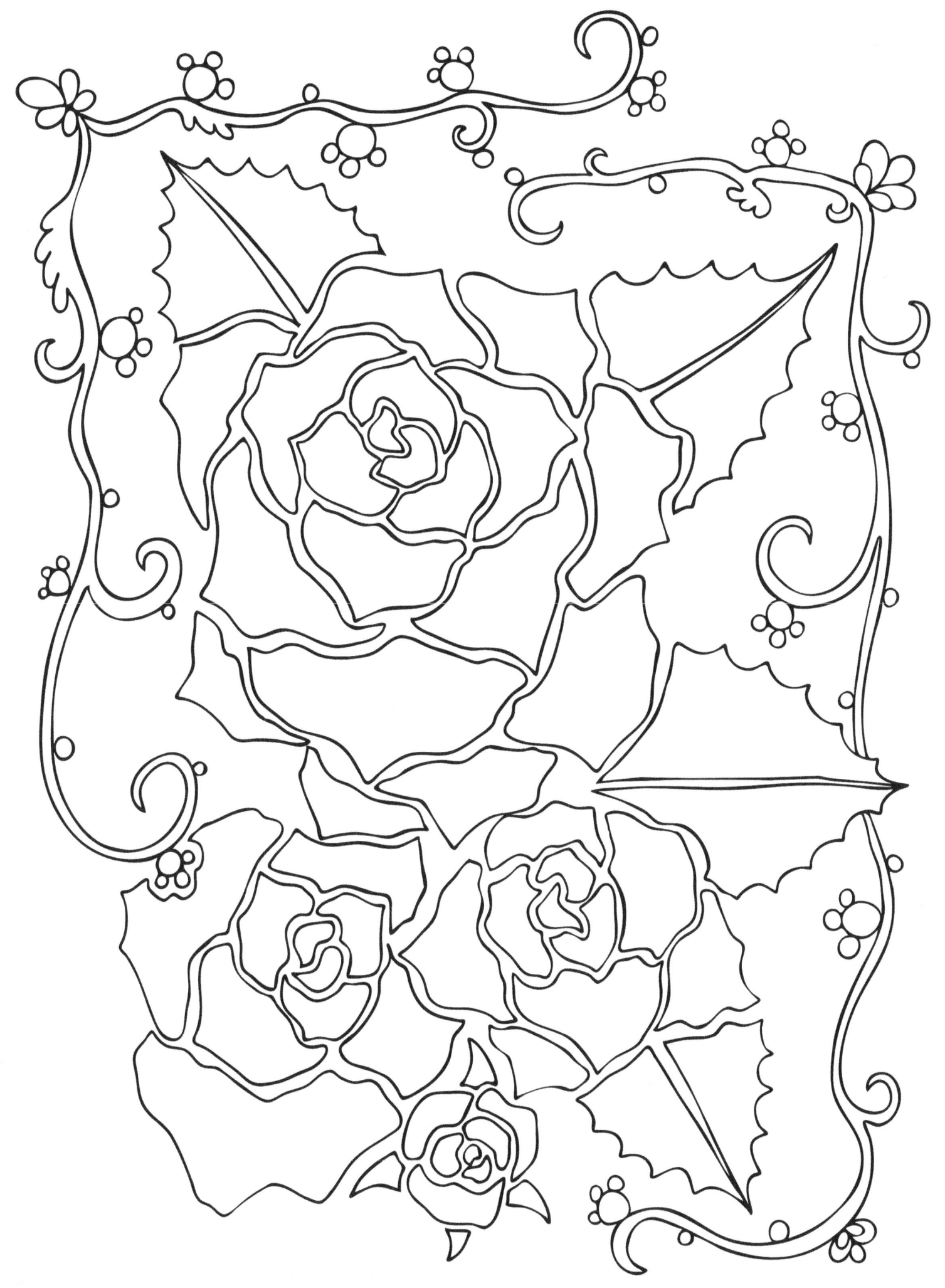

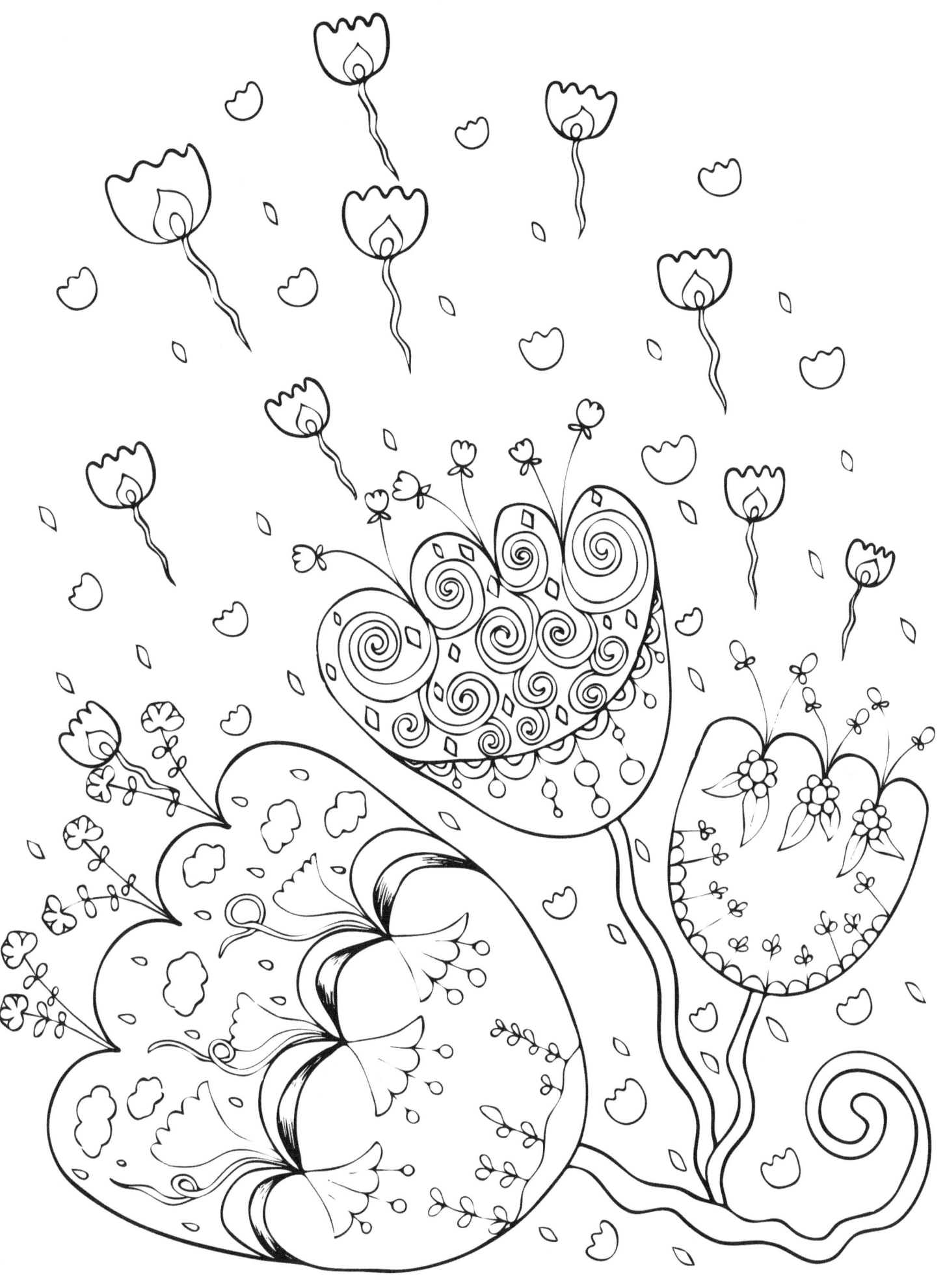

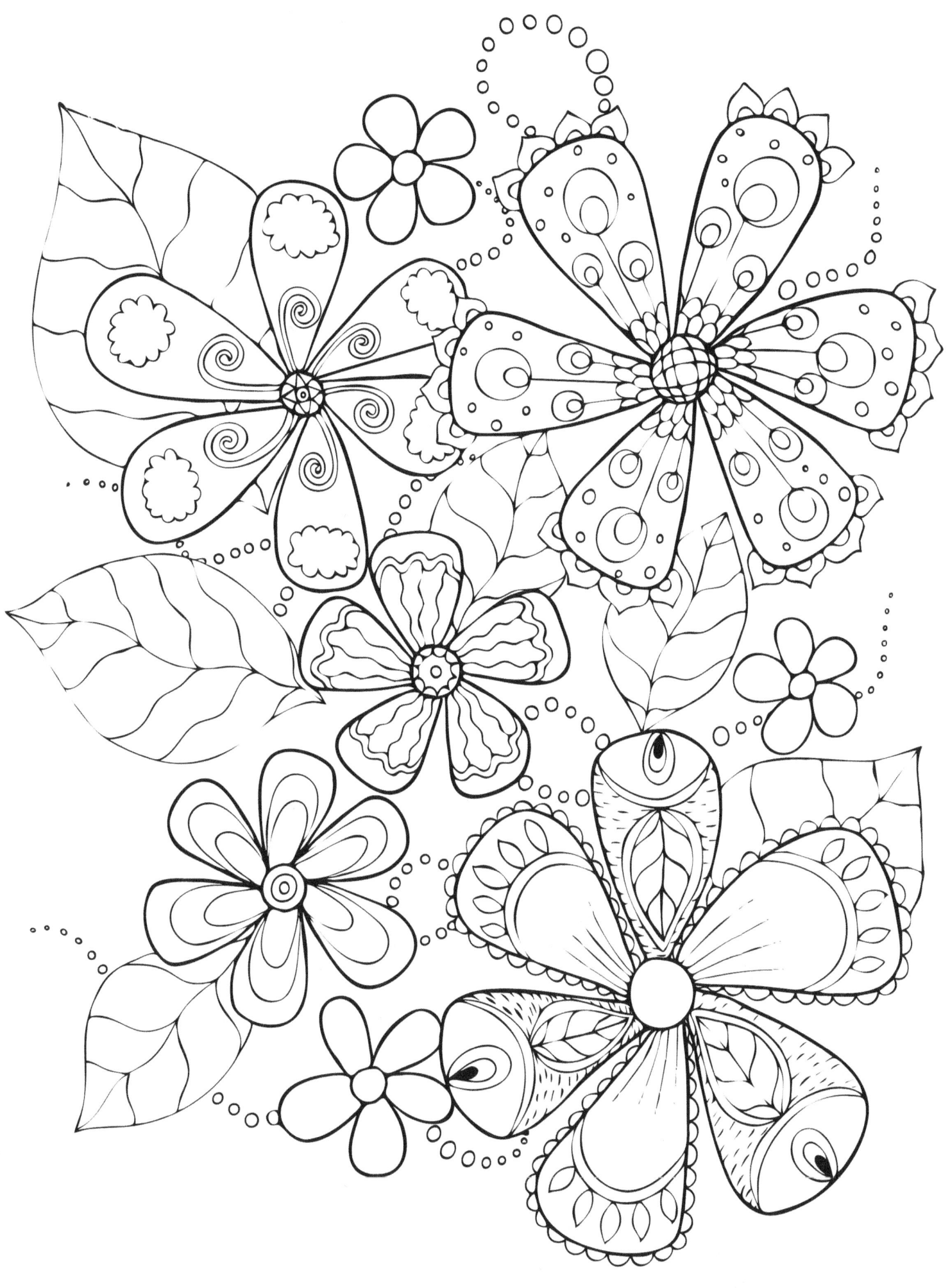

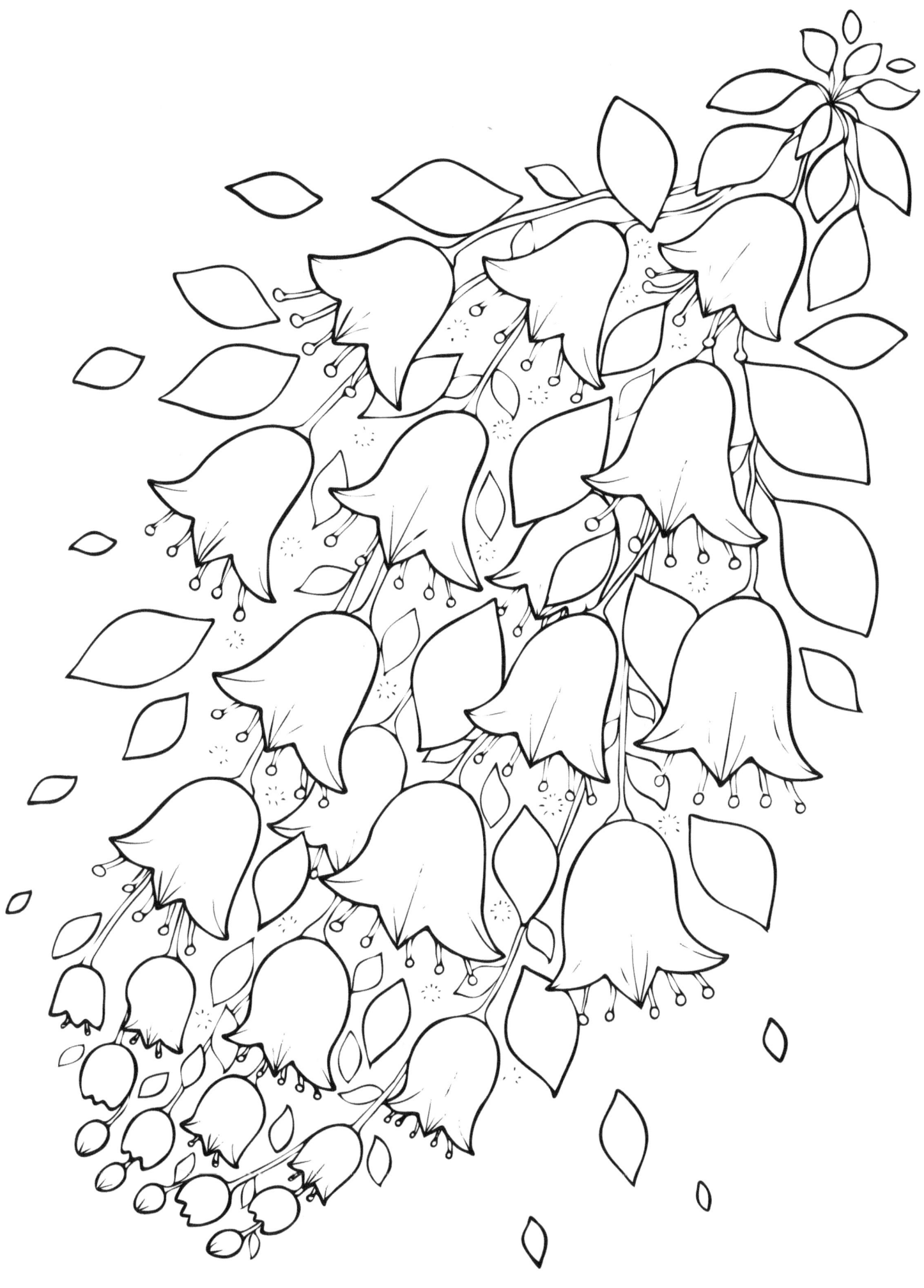

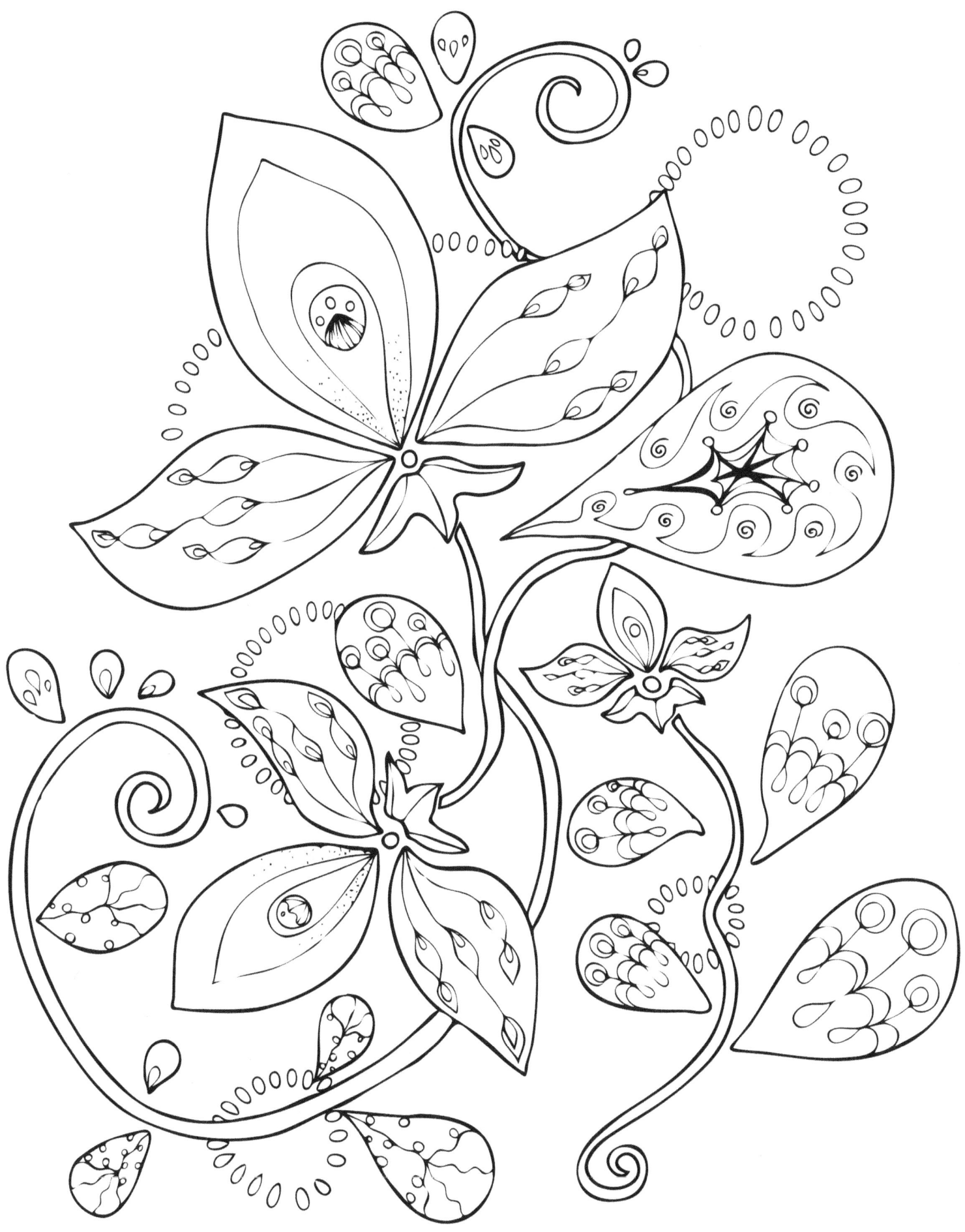

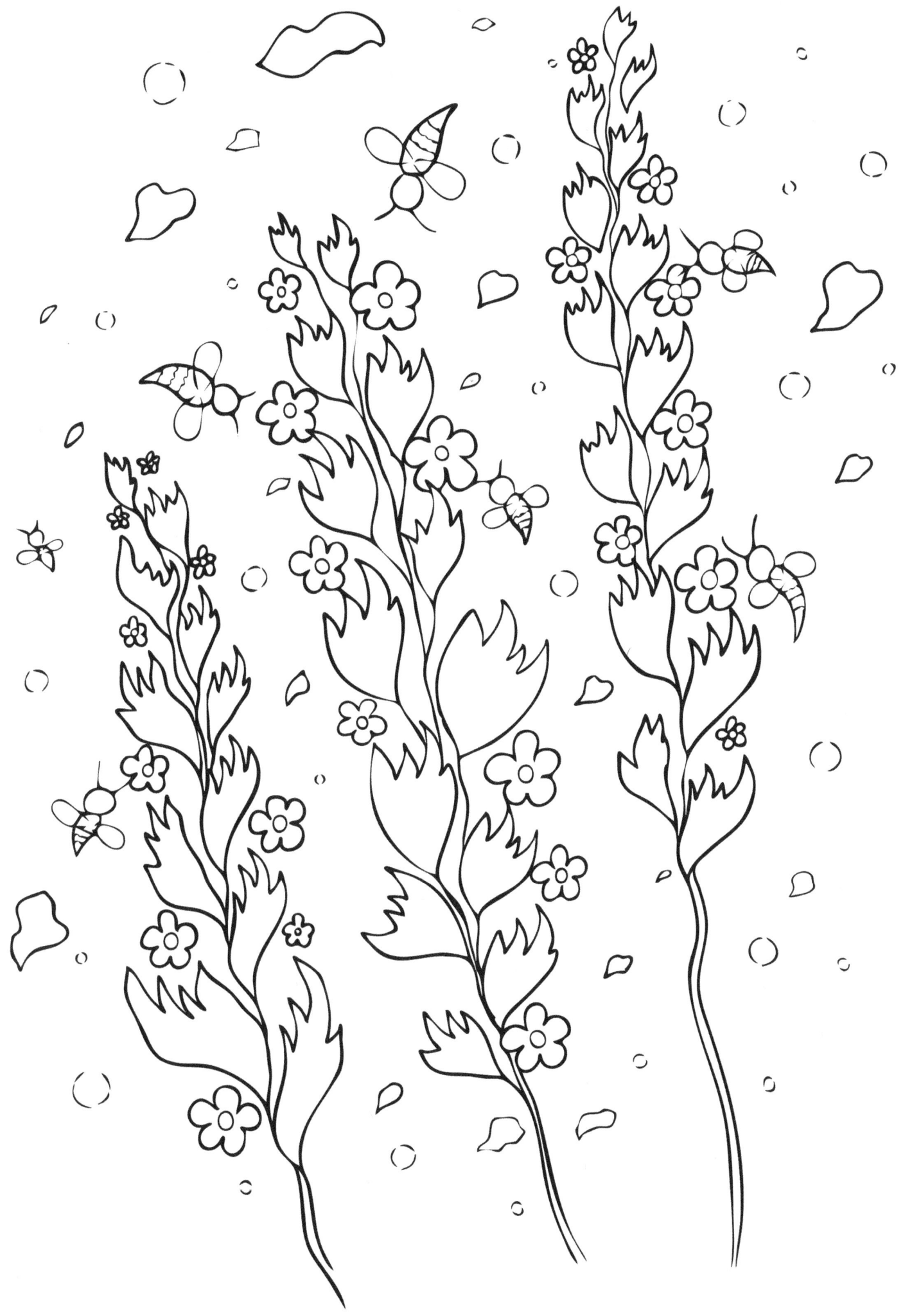

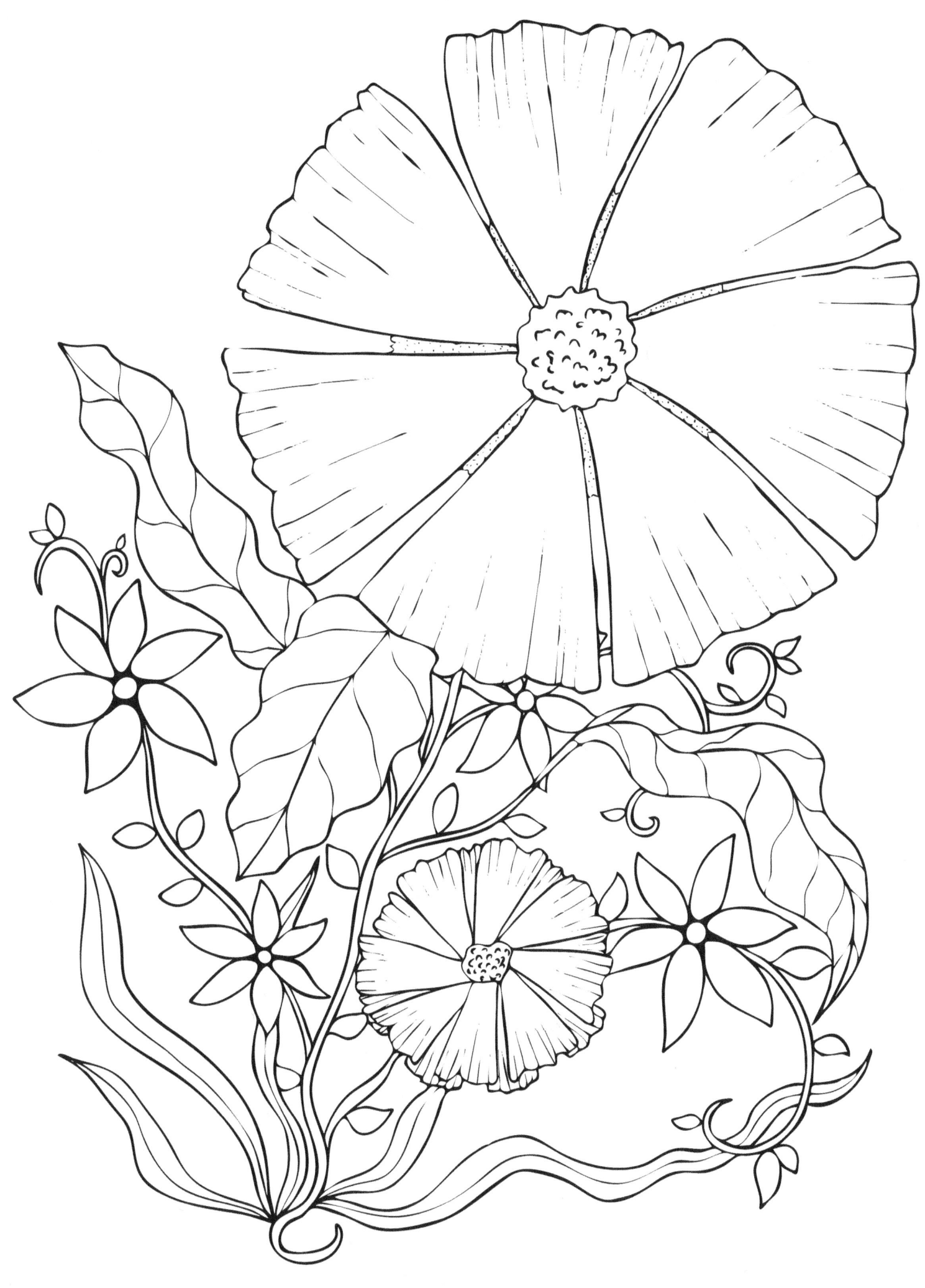

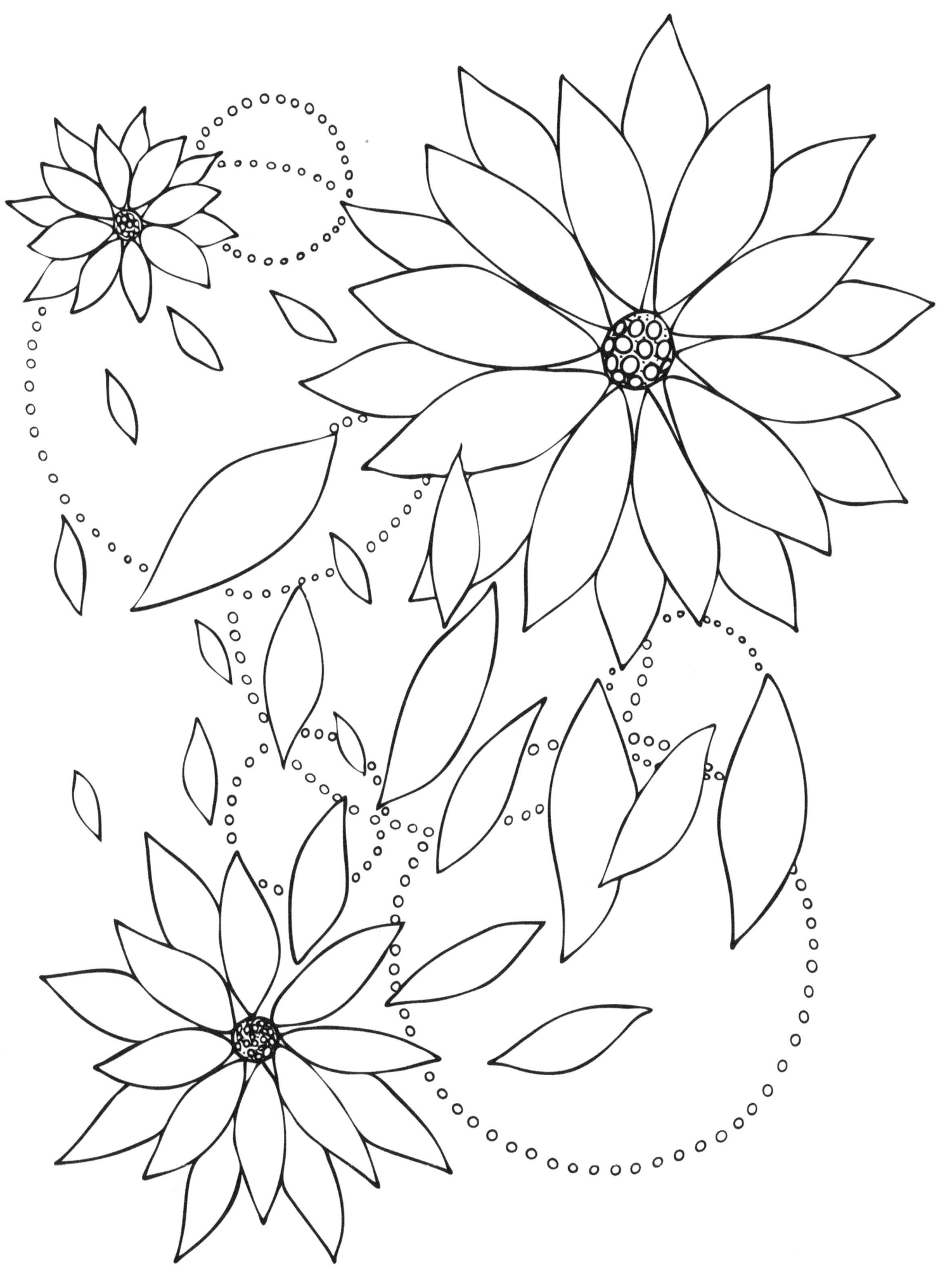

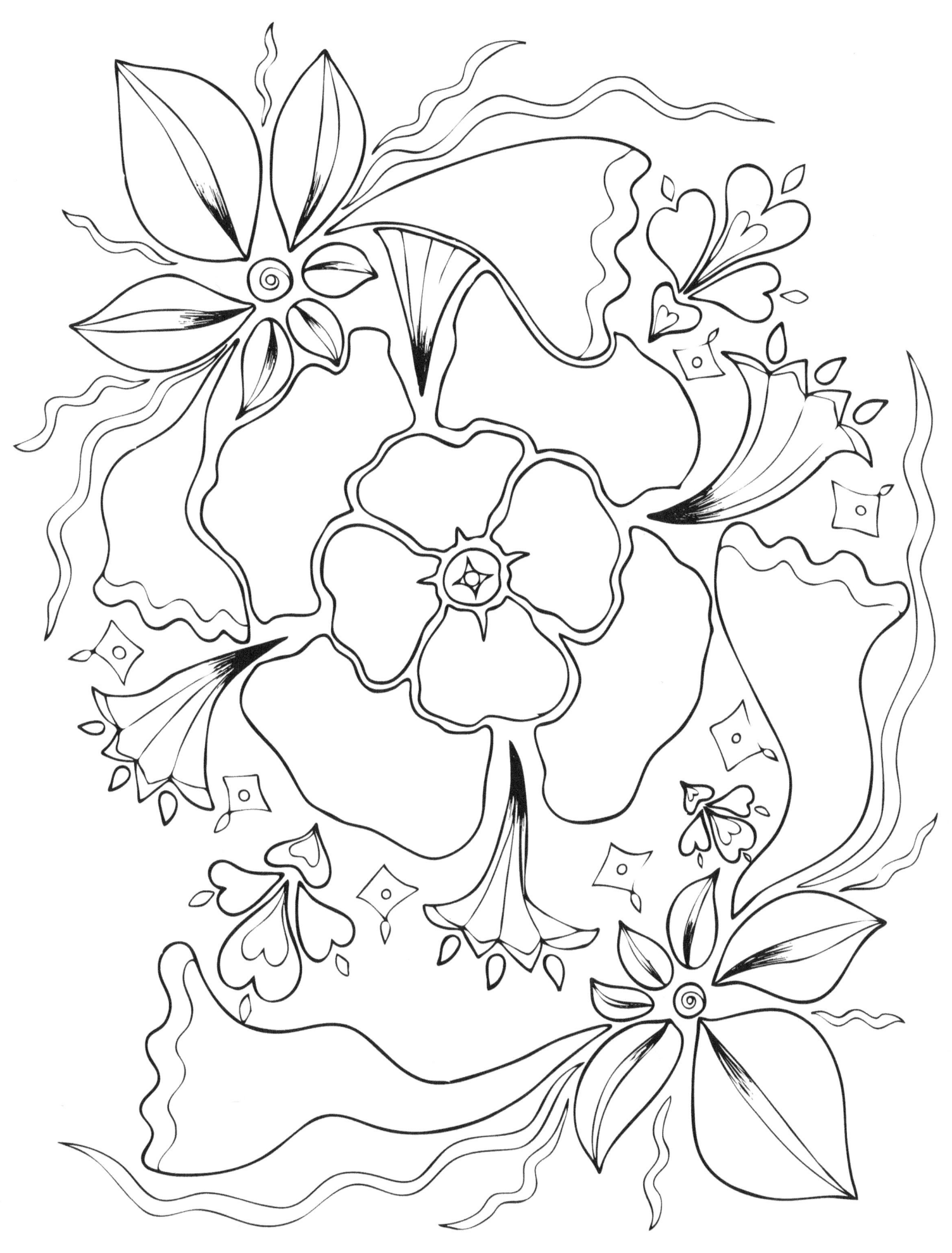